Highlights of Palmistry

Highlights of Palmistry

Heidi E. Kent
Master Palmist & Certified Medium

Illustrations by
Janice Maleyeff

IngramElliott

Highlights of Palmistry
Copyright © 2021 Heidi E. Kent

All rights reserved. No part of this publication may be reproduced, stored in a retrieval system, or transmitted in any form or by other means electronic, mechanical, photocopying, recording or otherwise, without the prior written permission of the publisher.

Published by IngramElliott, Inc.
www.ingramelliott.com
9815-J Sam Furr Road, Suite 271, Huntersville NC 28078

Book design by Maureen Cutajar, gopublished.com
Cover design by: H.O. Charles
Illustrations by Janice Maleyeff

ISBN Paperback: 978-1-952961-03-8
ISBN E-Book: 978-1-952961-04-5

Library of Congress Control Number: 2020948769

Subjects: Non-Fiction—Spirituality. Non-Fiction—Self-Help.

Published in the United States of America.
Printed in the United States of America.

First Edition: 2021, First International Edition: 2021

PUBLISHER'S NOTE: This book is designed to provide helpful information in regard to the subject matter covered. It is sold with the understanding that neither the author nor the publisher is engaged in rendering of any physical, psychological, emotional, financial, legal or other professional services. Neither the publisher nor the author shall be liable for any damages of any kind arising out of or caused, directly or indirectly, by your use or application of any information contained in this book. The publisher hereby disclaims all warranties of any kind, including any warranty of fitness for a particular purpose, and disclaims any and all liability for any errors, inaccuracies, omissions or any other inconsistencies herein. The content of this book is for informational purposes only and is not intended to be a diagnosis, recommendation or cure for any specific medical, psychological, emotional or spiritual problem or a substitute for consultation with a qualified physician, healthcare provider or other licensed professional. Please consult with your own physician, healthcare provider or other licensed professional regarding the use and application of the information in this book. The publisher and the author make no guarantees concerning the level of success you may experience by following the advice, suggestions and recommendation contained in this book, and you accept the risk that results will differ for each individual.

Dedication

This contemporary volume is dedicated to my palmistry teacher Reverend Ellen McReyolds with great thanks; my business partner Marsha G. Cook for the great fun; and my beautiful Grands for all the joy.

Contents

Introduction 1

Working Hand and Hand of Destiny 11

Quality of the Hand 17

Sharing Information 21

Are You Independent? 27

To Spouse or Not to Spouse 31

The Life Line 33

The Sister Line 41

Are You Stubborn? (More Thumb Stuff) 45

Family Connection 51

The Heart Line 55

The Head Line 59

The Great Triangle and Quadrangle.	63
The Simian Crease	67
Career, Line of Destiny, Fate.	71
Marriage, Relationships, and Children	75
Mystic Cross and Travel	79
Health	83
Hands	87
Fingers.	91
Mounts.	97
Important Markings.	101
Keys of the Hand	105
Are You an Old Soul?	111
Gain the Upper Hand.	115
About the Author	119

Highlights of Palmistry

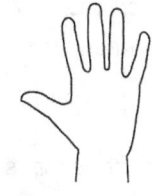

Introduction

This booklet is written as an introduction to the art of palmistry. It is a book of tidbits and simple shorthand rather than a complete, in-depth tome, and it includes basic illustrations depicting the important aspects of the hand. This will give you a quick method of exploring a being's strengths and weaknesses at a glance.

Palmistry's primary use is exploring an individual's identity. A palmist sees the hand as a map of the self, a physical expression of the inner you. Hands come in many shapes and sizes, and no two are ever alike. Each hand is totally unique and is a very personal signature. Palmistry is far more than predicting the future; it is a way of understanding who you are.

As distinctive as a genetic code that sets us apart from every other individual on the planet, each human hand contains its own unique and personal story. Palmistry offers the complete personality profile of an individual, including his or her major life choices, challenges, and opportunities. Using the hand as a tool to learn more about an individual is as old as human curiosity. You don't have to be psychic or clairvoyant to learn this art.

When a professional palm reader looks at your hand, he or she is looking for patterns and answers to the great questions of life. Will you find love? What kind of career might you choose? How successful will you be? Will you enjoy good health throughout most of your life?

Your hands contain helpful information about your talents, emotions, dreams, and spirituality. It is important to always remember that they are like a roadmap full of many choices that can affect your destiny. However, within your lifetime, it will be up to you to decide where you want to go!

The lines on your hands keep changing over time. Just as your life keeps changing, so the lines on your palm will move and alter to reflect those changes. With the help of palmistry, you can embark on your life's journey with a map of your destiny in the palm of your hand. Do you have the courage to explore your palm and the palms of those in your life?

HISTORY

The origins of palmistry (like the origin of the other divinatory arts (astrology, the tarot, and the I Ching) are shrouded in antiquity. All we know is that palmistry precedes written history, for when history is first recorded, it is already a highly advanced art.[1]

Palmistry is said to have originated in India, and then spread throughout China before finding its way to Egypt, Greece, and the rest of Europe. Interestingly, despite its suppression in the Middle Ages and its prohibition during the reign of King Henry VIII (who banned palmistry and other alternative practices, branding those who used it as sorcerers and devil worshipers), it still flourished. What is certain is that palmistry has been used since the earliest times as a means of reading history, of divining the future fortune and fate of the one presenting the hand. Its earliest practitioners are said to have been Chaldean magicians, the Priests of Isis in Egypt, and the Brahmins of India.[2]

Palmistry is as old as the days of Job. Job was an ancient book, probably a classic by the time Moses wrote Genesis and the law (the Ten Commandments). In former times, palmistry ranked among the learned arts and was recognized as one of the sacred and peculiar gifts. It was studied and practiced by the philosopher, the priest, and the Oracle, among whom it was an esoteric accomplishment and a much-prized possession.

Palmistry was a highly respected art among Greeks and Romans, who devoted many volumes to the subject; Homer is said to have written a treatise, named *On the Winds of the Hands*. This lost manuscript is frequently referred to by later Greek writers. Aristotle's work on the subject, which he is supposed to have presented to Alexander the Great, is, however, indisputable.[3]

During the Middle Ages and the Renaissance, palmistry reached one of the highest points of its popularity. The Comte de St. Germain, a nineteenth-century occultist, notes, "Works on palmistry were penned by alchemists and astrologers, the profound Arabs as well as the Italians, the Dutch, the Germans, the French, and the English."[4] With the dawning of the age of reason in the seventeenth century, widespread public interest in palmistry died out, and few distinguished works were produced during this period. The art was kept alive by the mysterious nomadic group known to the general public as Gypsies. Fortune-telling is universally practiced by the Gypsy women, among whom it is considered a tradition and exact art.[5] It was another 200 years, in the 1800s, before palmistry, along with the other divinatory arts, was to enjoy a resurgence.

My Story

For me, it all started on a dark and rainy night when I arrived at Camp Chesterfield, a metaphysical community in Chesterfield, Indiana. Entering the grounds, I spotted the camp's hotel. I was told by the desk clerk that I had booked the last room. The woman at the front desk directed me to the chapel, where a service had just begun. I thanked her and said I would go the next day. She insisted I drop my bag at the desk and go immediately to the chapel.

The chapel service was nice and, since I was last to arrive, I was first out. At the bottom of the chapel stairs stood an elderly lady.

As I smiled at her, she took my arm and said, "Dear, are you going to the séance?"

"Séance?" I replied. "Where is that?"

And thus, I started my adventures in forms of mediumship, including palmistry. Ultimately, I ended up living "on camp" and going to Miss Ellen's palmistry class every Tuesday afternoon for two years.

The truth about what drew me to palmistry is that I am a very curious soul and personally want to know everyone's deepest, darkest secrets. By simply shaking a person's hand, you are introduced to that individual's vibration; by grasping their arm, you can interpret their soul's energy, and by reading their palms, you are able to explore every little nuance the rest of the world cannot see.

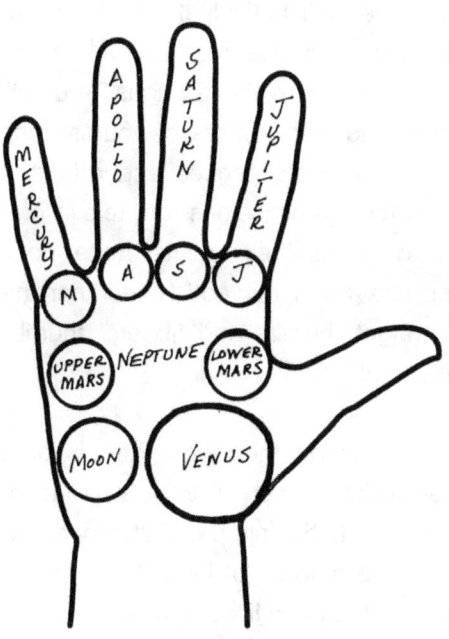

The Plan

This handbook is written for the individual who is interested in themselves and others. Because palmistry can be a complex study, I have attempted to encapsulate each idea in a simple picture. Picture by picture, you can analyze the lines, colors, and mounds of the hands to determine their individual meanings, thereby conveying insights into the reading of palms, wrists, and fingers. As you turn these pages, you will discover the strengths and weaknesses of yourself and your family, as well as your colleagues and others. For example, when watching politicians on television waving their hands to make their points, take notice. Are their thumbs straight or curved? Remember that truth tellers have straight thumbs and fibbers' thumbs are curved. Enough said!

While working on the layout of this book, I have attempted to introduce you to various facets of the hand. Beginning with the shape of the hand, which in itself gives a huge amount of individual information, we then travel on to the main lines of the palm, which explain the ideas of the hand. The hand of destiny, usually the left hand, reflects the goals and challenges of this life, while the right hand works on the realities of present time. Finally, we discuss the mounts, marks, and surface areas that give a more finite picture.

It is my hope that, working with this little book, you can investigate individual situations while holding a basic tool—*the hand*.

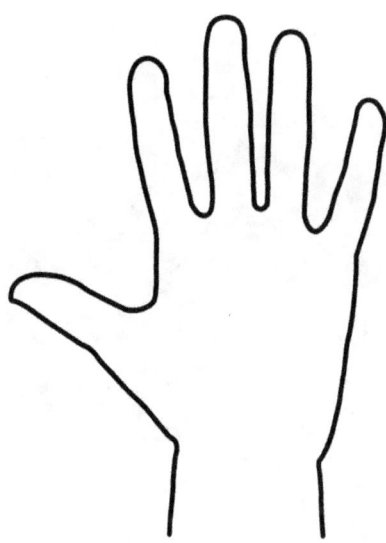

CHAPTER 1

Working Hand and Hand of Destiny

RIGHT-HANDED VS. LEFT-HANDED

The hand with which you write is known as the dominant hand. This is your **working hand**. The working hand may also be known as the working palm. For most of us, this is the right hand.

The alternate hand is known as the least dominant or **passive hand**, which charts your destiny. The passive hand may also be known as the **hand of destiny**. For most of us, this is the left hand.

If you are left-handed, consider the working and passive hands in reverse.

Of fundamental importance when assessing the hand, the issue of right- and left-handedness should be noted. Considering modern anatomy, the hand can be viewed as an endpoint of nerve impulses coming from the brain. Therefore, the constant motion of nerve impulses can be the direct cause of lines and creases. It is this indirect channeling of a person's feelings, wants, needs, actions, and unconscious mind (all registered and stored in the brain) that makes up the substance of palmistry. This implies that the palm lines may be directly influenced by a part of the mind that knows more about us and our direction in life than we care to, or are able to, admit.

Some palmists (including me) feel strongly that the will and the divine mind cooperate in etching lines that bear the importance of your destiny onto the palm. I usually tell my clients that the dominant hand changes every six months. Since a person's personality undergoes continuous change

HIGHLIGHTS OF PALMISTRY

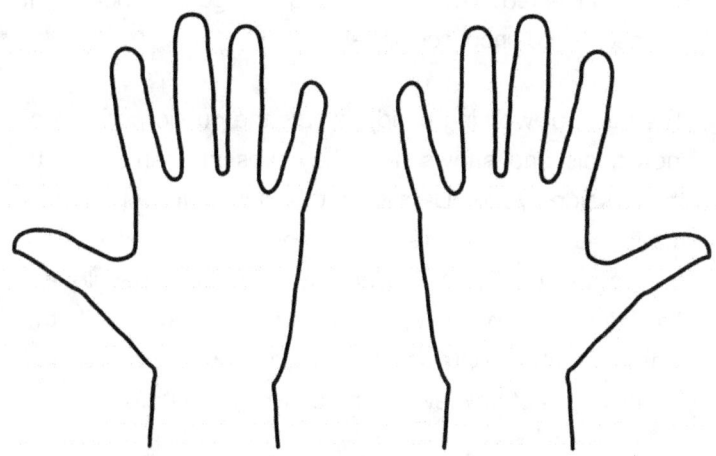

over a few years, the palms also undergo many changes, so palm lines come and go with time.

Practitioners of hand reading have long recognized that each palm registers and reveals different aspects of our lives. On right-handed individuals, the left (or passive hand) is associated with the private, intimate self and with imagination, instinctive reactions, natural aptitude, and potential abilities. This hand reveals information about childhood years, inherited tendencies, and congenital health. It represents the unconscious self.

The right, or working hand, reveals the public persona of individuals and shows how they present themselves to the outside world. Details in this hand will relay information about your reasoning powers, showing how talents are used and how potential has been developed. This dominant palm represents the conscious self, the mature adult. It contains information about our health and the progress of how events in our lives have unfolded.

Both hands should be examined together to see if the lines and marks on the two palms agree. If lines and marks agree, this adds greater certainty to whatever is indicated by the line or mark on each hand.

Where something is marked on the left but not on the right, the possibilities will exist in the subject's potentials but might never come to fruition. Where the two hands are exactly alike, the subject has not digressed in any way from his heredity or his agreed-upon life plan.

What do we mean by destiny? My definition here is the predetermined, usually inevitable—or irresistible—course of events. One theory indicates your destiny is determined by you prior to your birth. You chart a course of events that, throughout your life, you experience one by one. You determine, for example, the type of family life you wish to experience, the potential number of pregnancies you may have, how many marriages you will have, your physical experience (health), and so much more.

The working palm will tell you about your present circumstances. By looking at your palm, you will be able to tell a lot about your individual and social personalities. Remember: the lines on your hands keep changing over time. Just as your life keeps changing, so the lines on your palm will move and alter to reflect those changes.

CHAPTER 2

Quality of the Hand

Hard vs. Soft

"Even in the simple act of shaking hands, one can form many conclusions about an individual's character."
Heidi E. Kent

While shaking a person's hand, one can absorb the **individual's energy**. Pay attention to the sensations you feel when shaking or holding hands. You may be able to sense the person's electrical output, which might range from sad to happy or from intellectual to hysterical.

These nuances of the hand can help you form conclusions about an individual's personality or character traits. They are an important, but subtle tool in palmistry and related arts.

- A soft hand often indicates a passive person and, possibly, an unmotivated person.
- A firm hand is a sign of an energetic, reliable nature.
- A very thin hand denotes a restless, energetic disposition, but one who is given to worry and fretting, and is generally discontented.
- The hand that feels listless in your grasp denotes a weak constitution that has only enough energy to live.
- A cold, clammy hand is a sign of poor health, generally a sensitive and nervous person.
- Persons who keep their hands closed while talking are distrustful by nature, have little self-reliance, and can seldom be relied on by others.
- A person who gives a firm grasp of the hand is self-confident, energetic, and generally reliable.

HIGHLIGHTS OF PALMISTRY

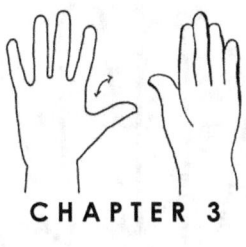

CHAPTER 3

Sharing Information

WORKING WITH THE THUMB

The placement of the thumbs shows the amount of personal information the individual shares with others. The deeper the thumb is set, and the closer to the hand it lies, the less the individual shares his or her innermost secrets with others. The wider the angle of the thumb, the more you will find the person to be open and honest. The thumb in itself is more expressive than any other member of the hand.

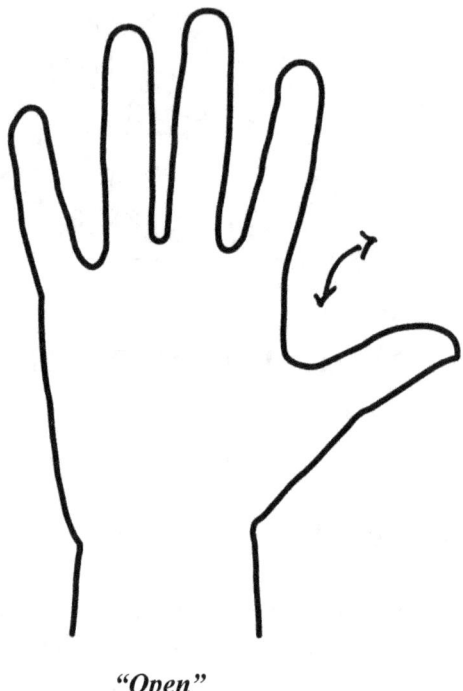

"Open"

A large, well-made thumb is the outward sign of a strong-willed, determined person, be they a man or a woman. The longer the thumb, the greater the will that rules the person's actions. The shorter the thumb, the more brute force and stubbornness sway the personality.

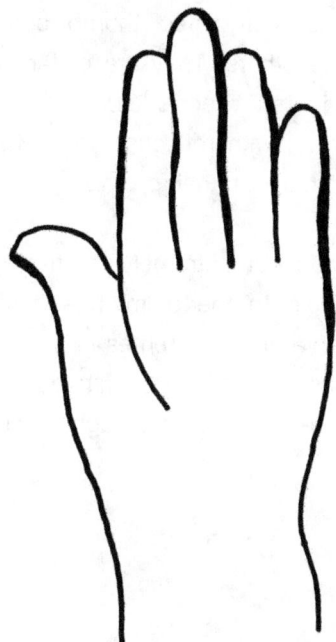

"Secretive"

Describing a person whose thumb is double-jointed (a thumb that bends backward): they are generous, adaptable to others, extravagant, and impetuous in their actions and decisions. They promise things quickly and are more often heard to say yes than no. But if they have time for reflection, they very often go back on their promises.

Individuals having a stiff-jointed thumb cannot easily adapt themselves to others. They are distant and more reserved with strangers. When asked to do something, they generally say no; with reflection they change their minds and rarely go back on their promises.

A thumb that stands out extremely far from the hand (almost at right angle to the palm) has difficulty with success. Such people go to extremes in everything they do, and many times are labeled as fanatics in religion, social reform, or whatever line of thought occupies their attention.

HIGHLIGHTS OF PALMISTRY

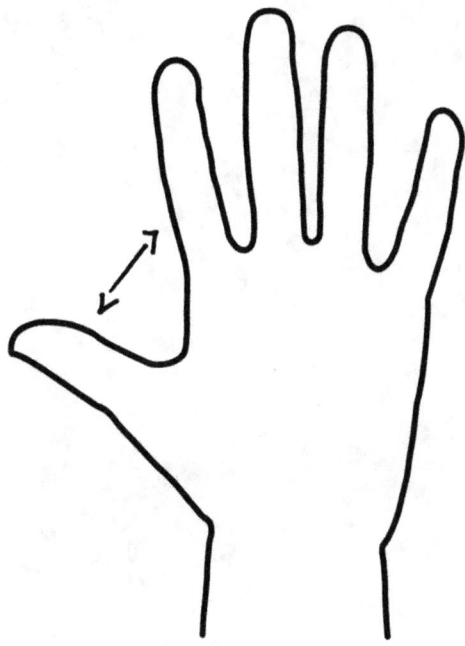

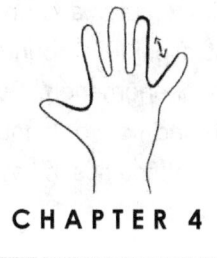

CHAPTER 4

Are You Independent?

THE LITTLE FINGER (MERCURY FINGER OR PINKY)

If your little finger, or **pinky finger** as it is sometimes called, cocks out from the other fingers at a great angle, your measure of independence is extreme and not always convenient for your friends, family, and acquaintances.

If the angles of the fingers are roughly equal, then your independent streak is well balanced. If the angle is quite close to the hand, then the individual has dependency issues.

If the pinky is long, it indicates a strong power of speech. The saying "to twist a person around one's little finger" originated from this phenomenon. Such people have a terrific gift of speech and flow of language. People with a short little finger have difficulties in saying what they want to say.

Louise Hay says that the little finger "represents the family and pretending." Some say that with a short pinky, you may be a part of the population who is shy. Many shy people are sensitive, and they truly make good friends.

The little finger is also called the **Mercury finger** and shows how creative or emotional you are. It represents communication skills, business savvy, diplomacy, and healing. The Mercury digit is a balancing power. It's easy to see why the word "Mercurian" is synonymous with the word "versatile."

HIGHLIGHTS OF PALMISTRY

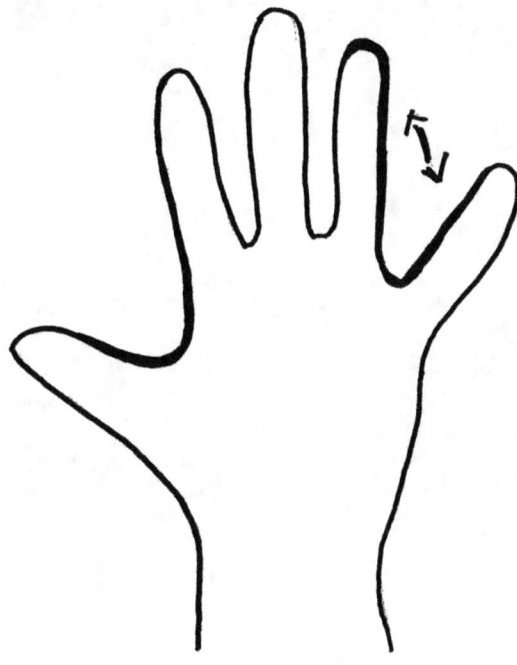

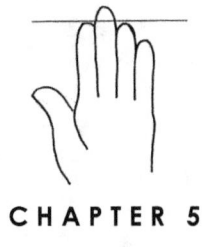

CHAPTER 5

To Spouse or Not to Spouse

Having the **first and third fingers** of equal length is the best sign of an equally balanced mind. Having these fingers of equal length in females means that these ladies will make contented wives. They will seek the security of marriage. If the fingers are not of equal length, it means that the individual will not be committed to a marital relationship.

With the male population, having equal fingers indicates strong commitment to a relationship. Once again, unequal fingers indicate a lack of commitment.

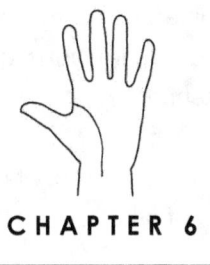

CHAPTER 6

The Life Line

THE CURVE OF THE LIFE LINE

The curve of the **life line** indicates the degree of generosity within an individual. When the line forms a wide semicircle that sweeps out to the center of the palm, it denotes an extroverted and exuberant person. The further the line sweeps, the more expansive the nature. If you have this type of line, you are interested in all that is going on around you.

When you see a life line that tightly hugs the thumb, most likely, you are an individual who is quite tight with your money, time, and attention.

A narrow arc indicates a person who prefers his or her own company to that of others.

The person with a middle-of-the-road curve is more than likely well balanced with time, money, and attention.

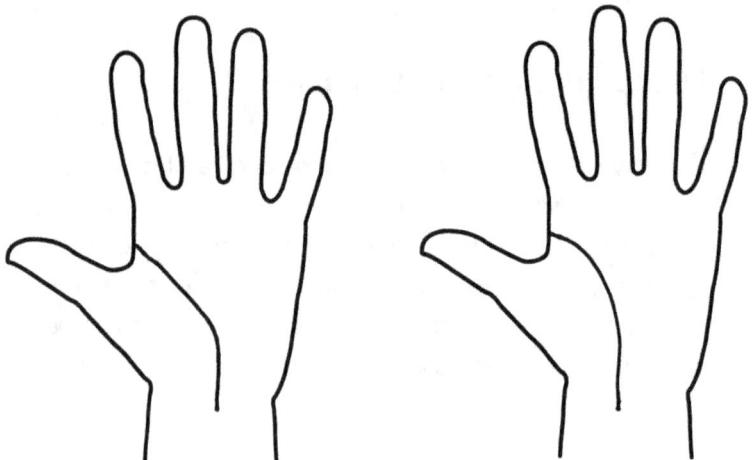

A strong life line denotes a more robust and vigorous constitution. If you have a well-etched line, you are tough, resilient, and you will cope with whatever life brings.

A weak life line, either because it is poorly constructed or because it appears light in comparison to the other major lines, or a line that is broken, denotes a delicate constitution and lowered vitality.

Within the life line is the **mount of Venus**. It is considered that people who have a natural bent toward being stingy are more likely to have a narrower arch, while those with a wider arch have a more generous nature.

Generally speaking, when the mount of Venus is large, it indicates a more passionate personality than when the mount is thin and narrow.

HEIDI E. KENT

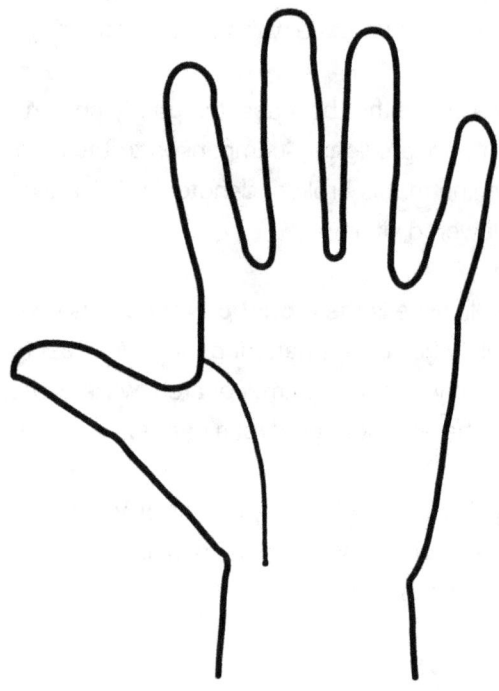

The Length of the Life Line

The length of the **life line** gives the individual's potential length of life. This is not the actual time of death. The life we are living is a life of free will. We get to work with our potential.

If one has an average eighty-year life line and consumes drugs and alcohol, their actual lifetime may be shorter. On the other hand, if a forty-year life line is shown, with a proper diet and exercise routine, the person can certainly extend their life beyond the forty years.

Where the life line is found with several ascending lines, even if they are small, this indicates a life of great energy. The dates in which these lines ascend from the life line may be considered lines in which the subject has made progress toward whatever may have been the special purpose of their destiny. If there are a series of markings on the life line, such as crosses, dots, or grills, then these extra markings are the indicators of special efforts or circumstances at different points in the person's life. For example, if, in your twenties, you went to law school, usually that sort of determined effort is recorded on the life line.

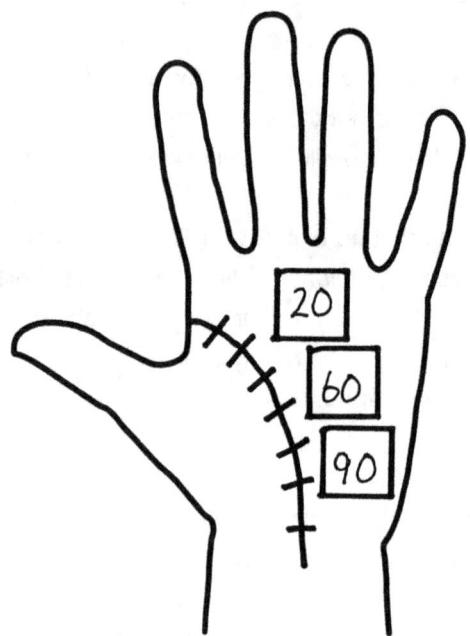

A long life line will not guarantee a long life, but it does show that its owner has considerable physical resources at his or her disposal. Providing the line is unblemished, it suggests that physical effort can be sustained over long periods. The difference between a long life line and a short one is that the owner of the long life line possesses greater stamina and resilience.

No other feature in the hand has labored under so much misconception or given greater anxiety than the short life line. True short life lines are rare. In such cases, a close inspection usually reveals that the hand puts out a fine branch that shoots out to the corner of the palm and connects with another line. This line represents a new section of the life line that takes over from the earlier one. Sometimes, the fate line does double duty and acts as a new section of the life line. Essentially, this formation denotes a major, positive change in the individual's life. Settling in a foreign country or inheriting a fortune are events that may be represented by an apparently short life line.

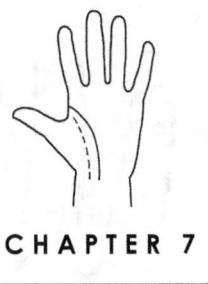

CHAPTER 7

The Sister Line

A SISTER LINE (ANY LINE THAT PARALLELS THE LIFE LINE)

You will find the **sister line** inside the **life line**, and it always denotes good news. A sister line strengthens and indicates spiritual protection and strong communication with the spirit world.

If it appears in both the right and left hand, it indicates that this is a karmic gift.

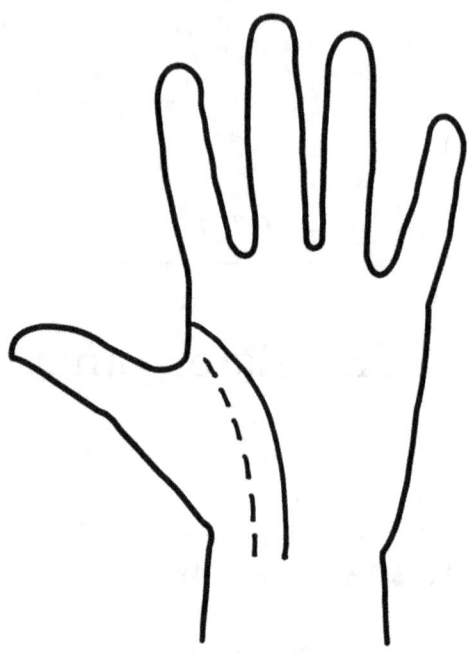

Sister lines define a degree of spiritual protection in the sense of physical strength and stamina. Sure, people with sister lines get sick—whether from incident, illness, or exhaustion—but they also recover quickly. A sister line is like having money in the bank: always useful and welcome.

When the sister line is strong or nearly as strong as the life line itself, it can indicate a high moral character. When the sister line is less than one-sixteenth of an inch away from the life line, you may have found a complex character who lives in two places at once, whether literally or figuratively. This sister line configuration may be found, for example, on someone who owns a home in town but spends weekends at the lake.

CHAPTER 8

Are You Stubborn? (More Thumb Stuff)

TESTING THE THUMB FOR FLEXIBILITY

If the thumb is **very firm**, with little back and forth movement, the individual is quite obstinate and unwilling to compromise. If the thumb is **movable**, then the person is flexible in their approach to life. If the thumb is extremely movable, then the person may be classified as extremely obliging in nature.

Sharing Information

The placement of the thumbs shows great amounts of personal information.

- The thumb is the most important digit in palmistry.
- The thumb represents character traits.
- The flexibility of the thumb is a measure of ability to compromise.
- The thumb can be straight or curved.
- The thumb has become a symbol, through the centuries, for *thumbs-up* which indicates that all is well.

The thumb is the most important feature of the hand for its ability to work in opposition to the fingers, placing human beings above all other animals. A truly opposable thumb has allowed human beings to grasp and manipulate tools and other objects in ways that no other mammal can.

The thumb is a principal key to the character of man. It represents behavior, purpose, vitality, willpower, reason, and logic. In Eastern palmistry, it is considered the most important digit in delineating character.

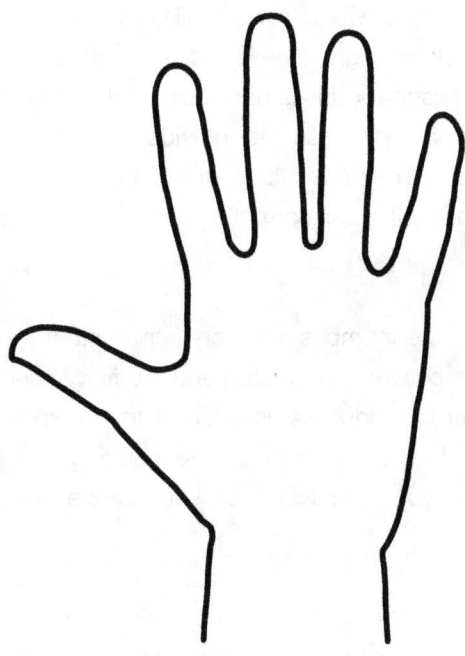

The right and left thumbs frequently differ, even if only slightly, so any assessment of the thumbs must be done with care. For example, a weak right thumb will be offset by a strong left one, or vice versa. So always check both thumbs carefully.

Oftentimes, people with great flexibility of the thumb are accused of taking a great deal of time to make up their minds. The reason for this is not because the individual is slow-minded, but because the individual is looking over the entire field. They are taking their time to make sure that they have all the information before they plan an event.

The setting of the thumb is also very important. If we have a wide space between the thumb and the first finger, then we know that the individual is open in their communications. Often, I'll say to clients, "We could go to lunch together, and you would tell me your deepest, darkest secrets."

In contrast, an individual who has a thumb remarkably close to the first finger keeps their personal information very private. If the thumb is rigid and immovable, that means more than just stubbornness; it accounts for rigidity in character and the inability to compromise.

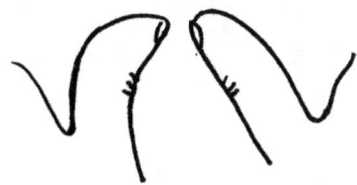

Perhaps one of the most critical factors of the thumb is whether it is straight or curved. Hold the thumb up and look to see if the thumb stands straight. This strongly indicates whether the individual tells the truth. If the thumb is curved away from the hand, the thumb indicates a liar. As you watch our politicians performing while waving their hands, please note whether they have straight or curved thumbs.

One of the topics we will explore with regard to the hand is the astrological naming of the fingers and thumb. The name of the thumb is **Venus**. If the thumb has a strong mount, then this indicates that the individual is sensitive, sensual, artistic, and/or has a dramatic flair. Other qualities we can attribute to the thumb are whether one is benevolent, affectionate, humble, and passionate.

CHAPTER 9

Family Connection

LINES ON HANDS—JOINING THE LIFE LINE AND THE HEAD LINE

This line refers to the nuclear family: your mother, father, and any siblings. If the **head line** and the **life line** are separated, the family connection is weak. If the lines are joined, the family connection is strong.

If the lines are joined, then the family connection is a strong one. The longer the joined lines (going into the palm), the stronger and longer the family connection.

HIGHLIGHTS OF PALMISTRY

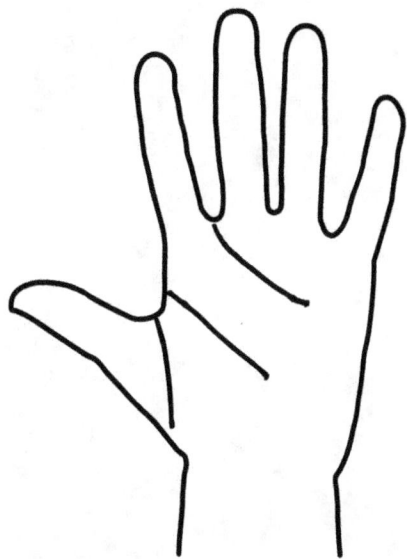

If the **head line** (the line running down the middle of the palm) and the **life line** are separated, then the family connection is impaired or weak. It means that the individual emotionally separated from his or her family exceedingly early in life.

CHAPTER 10

The Heart Line

How We Love

The **heart line** indicates how you love. There are many variations. For instance, a straight line indicates a romantic heart. A line which curves toward the fingertips indicates a more practical heart (decisions of love are not made on how cute the potential partner is, but rather on many different life factors).

The heart line runs across the hand under the fingers. It generally rises under the base of the first finger and runs off the side of the hand under the base of the fourth or little finger. The heart line relates to the affection, disposition, or temperament of the individual, as well as the mental side of the individual's nature.

The shorter the heart line is on the hand, the less manifest are the higher sentiments of the affections. A heart line that is extremely long denotes a terrible tendency toward jealousy.

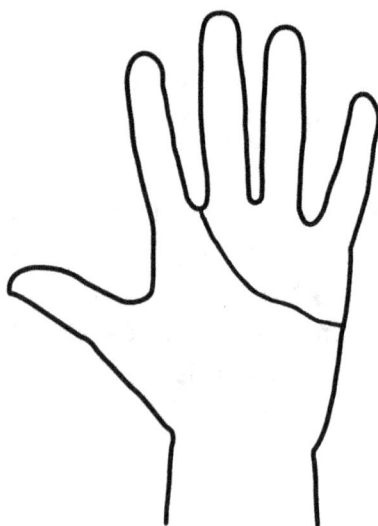

A heart line that is made up of a chain, or by a crowd of little lines running into it, denotes flirtations and an inconsistency in love. This seldom indicates any lasting affection. When the heart line is very thin and has no branches, it donates coldness and want in matters of the heart.

CHAPTER 11

The Head Line

HOW WE THINK

There are two major lines that run horizontally across the palm: the **head line** and the **heart line**.

The head line shows our mental and intellectual life—our psychological makeup and our intuitive abilities. It can also shed light on emotional difficulties as they influence mental health, as well as the physical condition of the head regarding such things as headaches.

The head line does not show how smart you are, but it can tell your palm reader how you think and where your skills lie.

A long head line shows intelligence, a good memory, a questioning spirit, and flexibility of interests, as well as the ability to reason and think logically. A deep and strong line means you can focus on problems and have a good ability to concentrate.

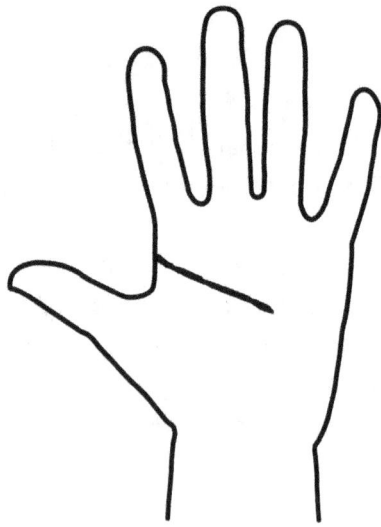

HIGHLIGHTS OF PALMISTRY

A short head line shows a mental world limited to practical matters with little imaginative flair, but it can also mean that your mental strengths are focused and concentrated in one area. The stronger the head line, the more focused you are, but a weak line shows inability to concentrate, and a tendency to daydream. Those who have a weak head line may be considered to be indecisive, unrealistic, or lacking in common sense. A wavy head line points to a person who is unsteady and unable to be trusted, and a fragmented head line shows a person who is worrisome, unfocused, or has a bad memory; they may also have a tendency toward having migraines.

CHAPTER 12

The Great Triangle and Quadrangle

THE GREAT TRIANGLE

The great triangle may be formed by the **head line, life line**, and **any third line**.

If you have a triangle in the center of your left hand it indicates that you have come into this life to lead a very spiritual life. Not necessarily a religious life, but a spiritual one.

This usually means that you put the interests of others ahead of yourself. The larger the triangle found on the hand, the greater the commitment. Looking at the working hand, the larger the triangle, the better job you have done with your spiritual life.

THE QUADRANGLE

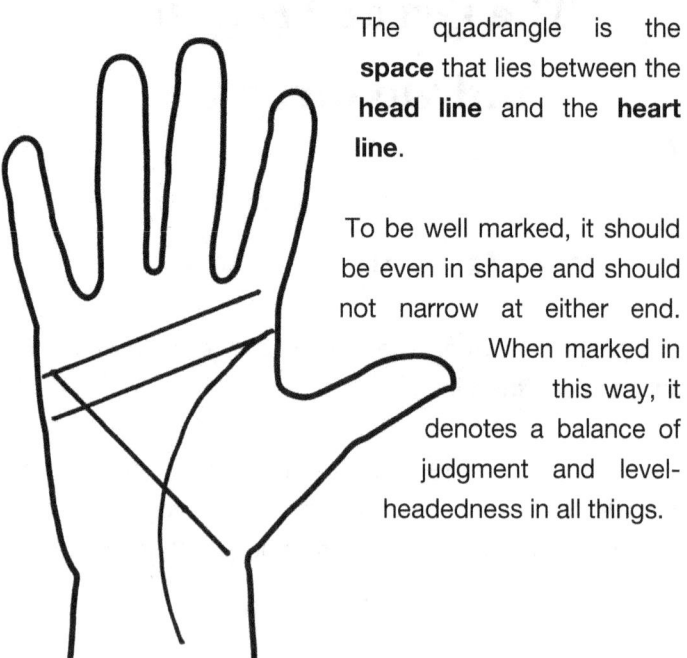

The quadrangle is the **space** that lies between the **head line** and the **heart line**.

To be well marked, it should be even in shape and should not narrow at either end. When marked in this way, it denotes a balance of judgment and level-headedness in all things.

The quadrangle represents a person's disposition or mental attitude toward other people. Where extremely narrow, it indicates the narrowness of views and bigotry in relation to religion. Where excessively wide, it suggests a lack of judgment in things and too much moral flexibility for the person's good.

CHAPTER 13

The Simian Crease

A FUSED HEAD LINE AND HEART LINE

The simian crease appears in the hand as a **fused heart line and head line**. When fused, they become one distinct channel that will run right across the palm from edge to edge.

It is found in a small percentage of typical hands, although it is also one of the features associated with some chromosomal disorders.

When found in a typical hand, the simian line signifies emotional intensity due to the fusion of heart and mind. If the crease appears on both hands, it can indicate a career criminal or career minister.

People with the simian line tend to be complex, forceful, and goal-oriented, but also jealous and egocentric.

HIGHLIGHTS OF PALMISTRY

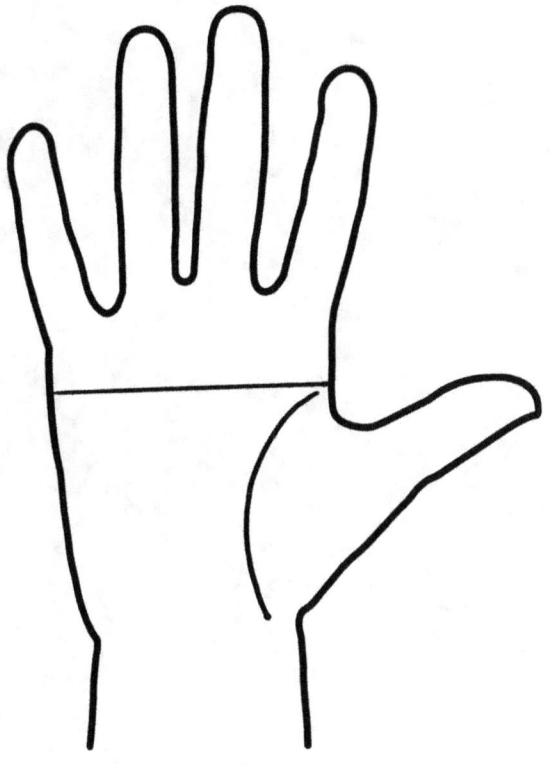

CHAPTER 14

Career, Line of Destiny, Fate

This line is known as either the **career line**, the **line of destiny**, or the **fate line**. It begins somewhere in the middle of the palm.

Depending on where the line starts, it indicates the type of work or career you decided on before you were born. Compare both your working hand (your dominant hand; usually your right hand) and your opposite hand (known as the hand of destiny). If, in your working hand, the line follows the same course as your hand of destiny, then you are achieving just about what you had hoped to achieve. If the line in your working hand is different than your hand of destiny, with free will, you have changed your mind about your career.

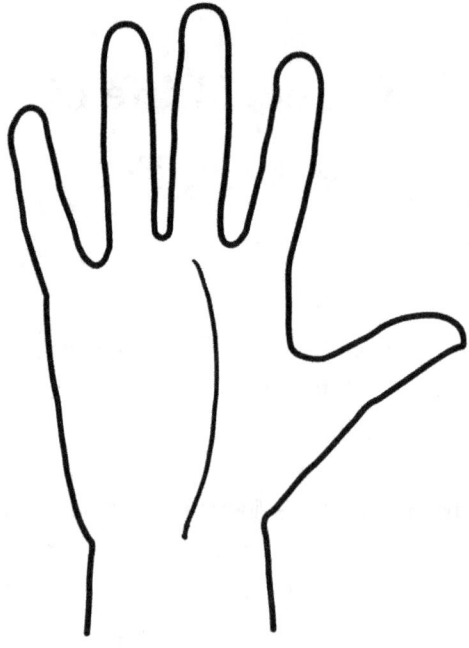

This line may be found on the hand at the moment of birth, clearly indicating the destiny that lies before you in the distant future. Another interesting phenomenon is when the career line descends on the right or left hand and stops, only to jump to a neighboring line. This indicates that the person has completed one line of work and has started a whole new line.

If there is no line in the middle of your hand, then you decided at birth that you would not have a standard career in this life. You did not come to experience a "career." While it does not mean that you will not support yourself, you came to experience "experiences."

CHAPTER 15

Marriage, Relationships, and Children

MARRIAGE AND RELATIONSHIP LINES: A SOLID COMMITMENT OF THE HEART

In the hand, the lines of relationship and marriage have only to do with solid commitments of the heart. For example, if you were legally married four times, not all these lines may appear on the palm. They appear only if there was a firm connection with your heart.

The universe does not recognize a piece of paper or wedding license at the courthouse, only the commitments of the heart.

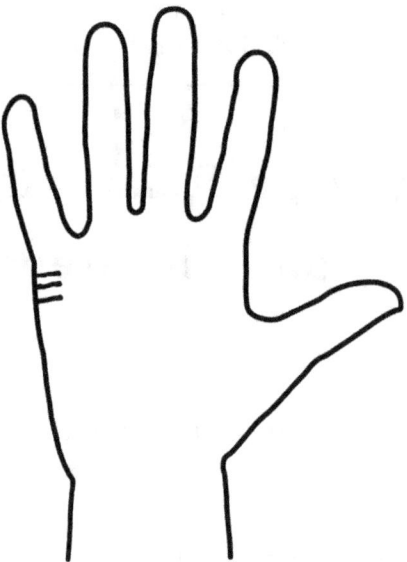

In the **less dominant hand**, the lines appear as potential relationships. If you have been in four committed relationships and you have five lines in this hand, it means there is the potential for one more.

Children

Potential Pregnancies in the Left Hand (Hand of Destiny), Actual Pregnancies in the Right Hand (Working Palm)

The lines indicating children are those finely marked, upright lines found immediately above the marriage lines; these lines can sometimes be extremely deeply etched.

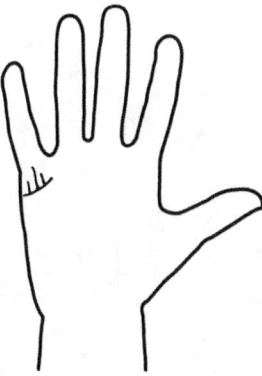

Broad and deep lines indicate boys, while fine and narrow lines indicate girls. To know the number of potential pregnancies, count the lines on the left hand. The right hand will reflect the number of actual pregnancies.

CHAPTER 16

Mystic Cross and Travel

THE MYSTIC CROSS: STRONG INTUITION

If the **crosses** are in the hand of destiny as well as in the working hand, then the individual has a genetic or family background with strong psychic potential.

THE MYSTIC CROSS: STRONG INTUITION

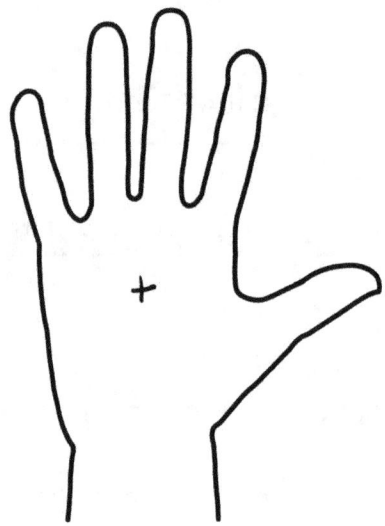

As with any other potential, an individual with these crosses must find a good mentor or teacher and practice, practice, practice, to develop it.

Travel (The Mount of the Moon)

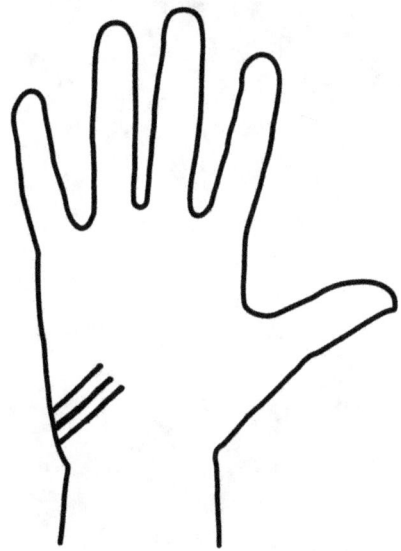

Usually, these straight lines start at the **curve of the mount** and travel toward the center of the palm. If there are no lines on the mount, it denotes the individual has little interest in travel. Many deep lines indicate a great deal of interest in traveling, or that actual travel is taking place.

CHAPTER 17

Health

HEALTH: DETERMINED BY PRESSING THE CENTER OF THE HAND

Take your thumb and your first finger, place the thumb in the middle of the palm, and squeeze. If the hand feels very firm, the individual is in good health. The softer the mid-palm feels, the less healthy the person.

Color is also important. If the palm has a pink blush, usually the individual has a chronic disorder such as asthma or diabetes. Very red hands are associated with a rise in blood pressure or with rheumatic conditions. Physiologically, they may signify glandular or liver problems. In a woman's hand, a reddish blush over the palm can be an early indication of pregnancy.

Cold, pale hands are linked to anemia or a temporary loss of iron. After menstruation, it may look as though the main lines appear white when the hand is stretched out. Listlessness often accompanies the pale hand. Shock can immediately drain hands of color, or sometimes turn the hand blue. An overall tan or rich color usually indicates good health.

HIGHLIGHTS OF PALMISTRY

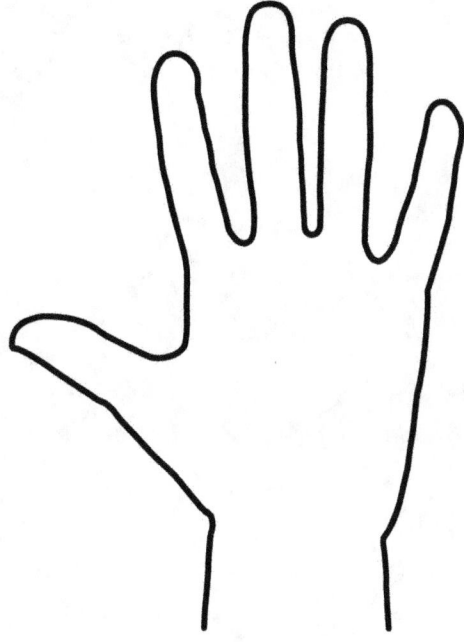

CHAPTER 18

Hands

A Full Hand

A hand covered in a cobweb of lines is known as a "full" hand. This is a sign that the nervous system is stretched and/or that its owner is high-strung. His or her imagination may run out of control, resulting in anxiety and psychosomatic disorders.

A Full Hand

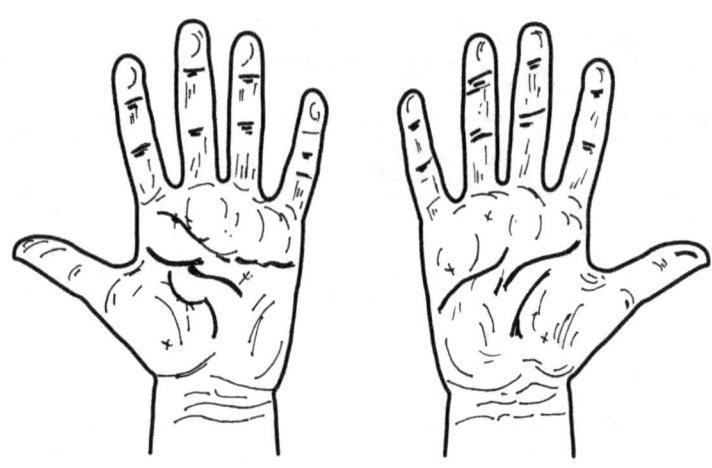

A hand covered in a cobweb of lines is known as a "full" hand.

An Empty Hand

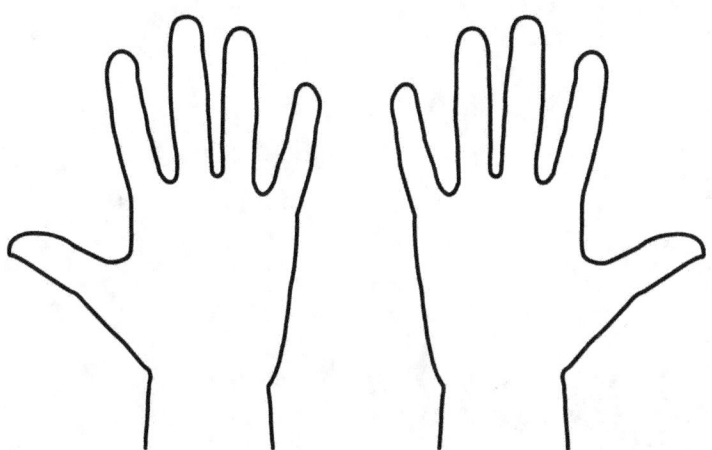

The "empty" hand contains only the major lines, and the palm is uncluttered. Here, the nervous system is balanced, and its owner can take the stresses of life in his or her stride.

CHAPTER 19

Fingers

EACH FINGER REPRESENTS A MYTHIC CHARACTER

Each finger represents a different area of life and is traditionally named after one of the mythological beings: Jupiter, Saturn, Apollo, and Mercury, whose characteristics express the digit's area of influence. The size and shape of each finger show the extent to which a person possesses the qualities it represents.

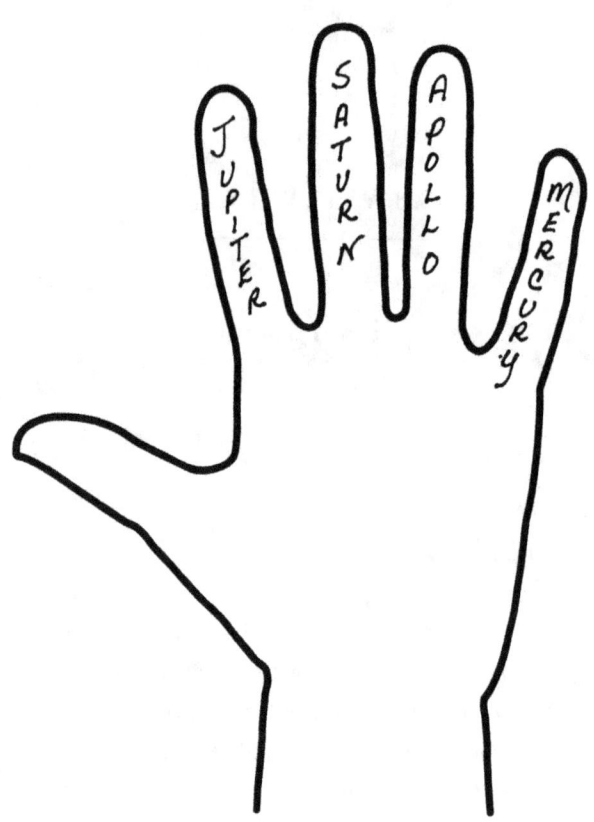

Jupiter—the index finger. In classical mythology, Jupiter was the chief god and ruler of the world. Traditionally, the index finger is named after him because it represents ego, leadership qualities, and one's position or standing in the world. Your assertiveness and ambition are shown here. A straight index finger denotes integrity. A very long index finger shows bossiness, while a short index finger shows timidity and self-doubt.

Saturn—the middle finger. This finger is named after Saturn, the father of Jupiter, and is associated with wisdom. This finger reveals how you deal with responsibility and whether you have a serious or careless attitude toward life. A long middle finger suggests an industrious mind, but also that humor may be lacking. If the middle finger is short, it denotes an irresponsible personality.

Apollo—the ring finger. Apollo was the sun god and is traditionally associated with music and poetry. Your ring finger reflects your creativity and sense of well-being. A strong ring finger is often seen on the hands of entertainers and artists. A weak ring finger suggests a lack of creative talent, while an excitingly long ring finger may reveal a gambling instinct.

Mercury—the little finger. Mercury, the messenger of the gods, is associated with communication. This finger reveals your powers of self-expression, and the longer it is, the more articulate you are likely to be. A short Mercury finger suggests you may have difficulty putting your thoughts into words. Traditionally, a curved little finger indicates shrewdness, but can also denote untrustworthiness and deceit.

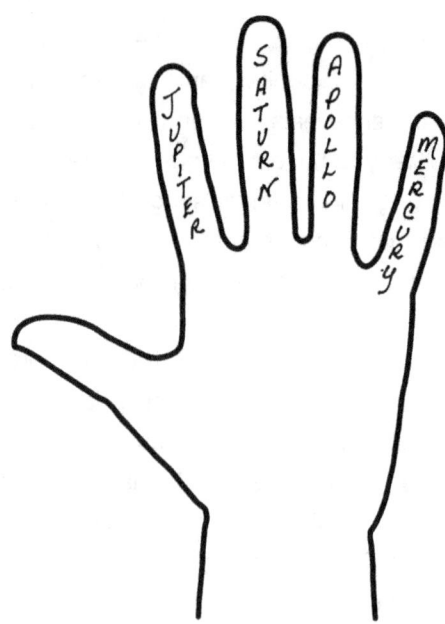

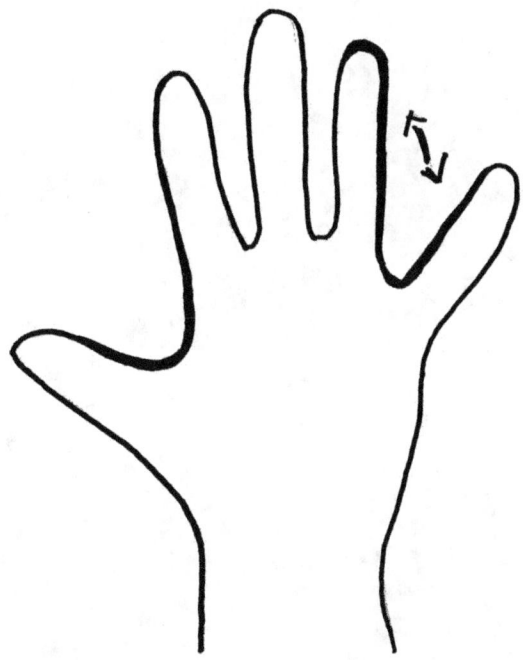

MERCURY FINGER STANDING APART

A wide gap between the Apollo and Mercury fingers shows independence; people with this formation do not like to feel hemmed in, either physically or psychologically.

CHAPTER 20

Mounts

MOUNTS: STRUCTURES OF EMPHASIS

Each mount represents a store of energy by its shape and construction. It suggests the strengths and weaknesses of the owner and the qualities associated with that mount. To determine whether a mount is overlarge and well developed or lean, you need to compare it to the other mounts in the hand. For instance, a lean hand will have relatively lean mounts, but one or two may be large or small in comparison with the rest.

HEIDI E. KENT

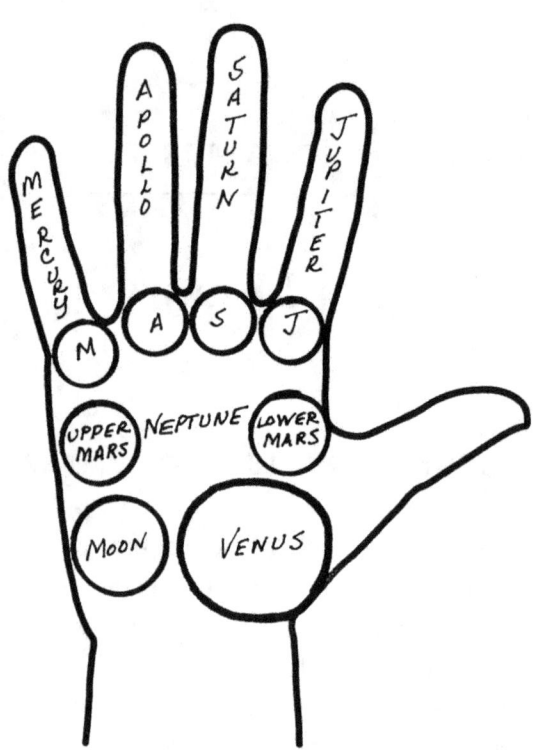

Under each of the five fingers rests a mount. Each of these mounts is named for its corresponding finger.

Mount of Venus (Thumb)—Indicates passion for romance as well as materialistic possessions.

Mount of Jupiter—Lies just below the index or first finger and indicates leadership, education, love, wisdom, and good friends.

Mount of Saturn—Lies below the middle or second finger and indicates a quiet but skeptical nature.

Mount of the Sun—Lies below the ring finger or third finger and indicates creativity, success, beauty, and talent.

Mount of Mercury—Is situated below the little or fourth finger and indicates communication, art in the form of poetry, and an inborn talent for eloquence.

CHAPTER 21

Important Markings

MARKINGS ON THE HAND HAVE SPECIFIC MEANINGS

Islands reduce the promise of the lines or mounds on which they are found; an island on any mount weakens the qualities the mount expresses.

Dots are a sign of a temporary stop of that activity. Dots on the line weaken it and arrest its growth.

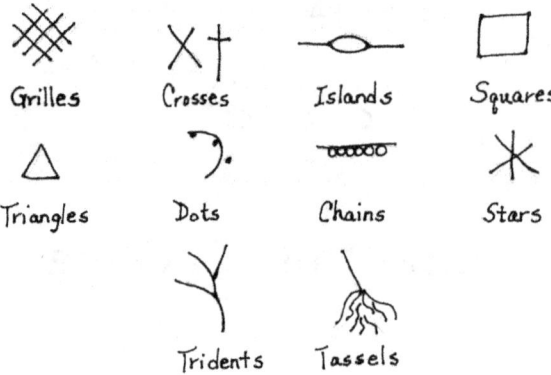

Grills denote difficulties and obstacles in connection with whatever the mount represents and lack of success in whatever quality or talent the mount symbolizes.

Star is the most fortunate mark to possess. If the star appears in your left hand, it indicates a great wish, miracle, or success has been awarded to you. When the act is delivered, the star then appears in your right hand.

Square is usually called the mark of preservation; it indicates escape from danger at that particular moment.

Chains indicate a lack of force or fixed direction of purpose.

CHAPTER 22

Keys of the Hand

The keys of the hand include the Girdle of Venus, the Ring of Solomon, the Ring of Saturn, and the Ring of Apollo. The keys appear on different areas of the hand and are associated with specific personality traits.

GIRDLE OF VENUS

This marking denotes an individual with intense feelings, heightened emotions, and sensitivity. The girdle proclaims creative talents and responsiveness to others. It also shows a tendency to get easily hurt and to overreact emotionally.

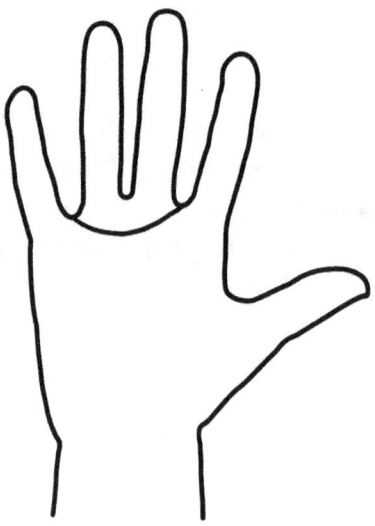

RING OF SOLOMON

The Ring of Solomon is found on the mount at the root of the Jupiter finger. Associated with the fabled judgment of Solomon, when present, it represents wisdom and philosophical understanding.

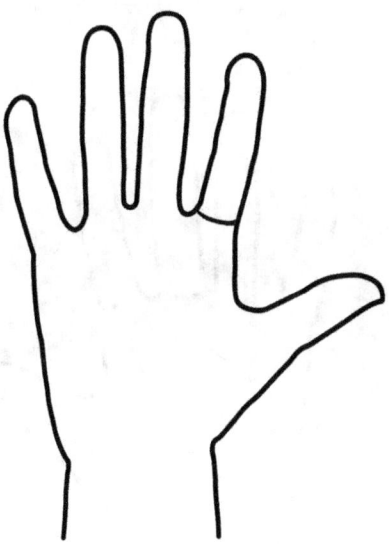

Ring of Saturn

The Ring of Saturn circles the root of the Saturn finger; it is the classic symbol of the wet blanket or party pooper. If you have a Ring of Saturn in your hand, you can work at making it disappear by thinking positively and taking a more lighthearted approach to life.

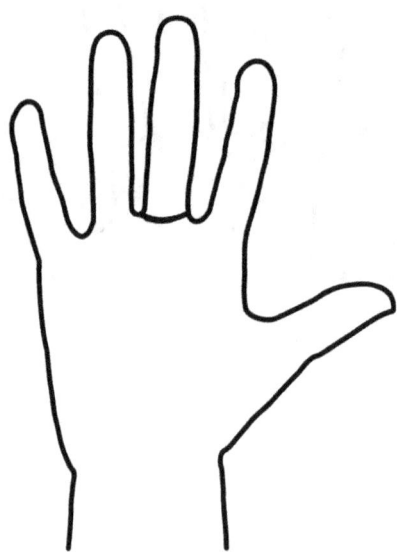

RING OF APOLLO

Located at the base of the Apollo finger, this ring is very rare and, when present, the marking seems to act as an emotional block, frustrating the natural spontaneity and the optimism of the individual. The Ring of Apollo can be made to disappear with a positive attitude. Taking opportunities to participate in cultural activities may encourage artistic inspiration.

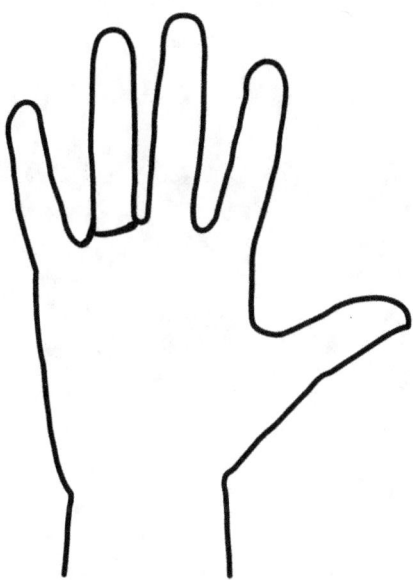

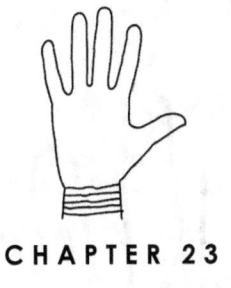

CHAPTER 23

Are You an Old Soul?

COUNT RASCETTE LINES

The bracelets, also known as rascettes or rascette lines, are a charming attribute that can lead to a greater understanding of what the person will face in this life. Every person has some form of a rascette on the hand, and it is located between the palm and the wrist.

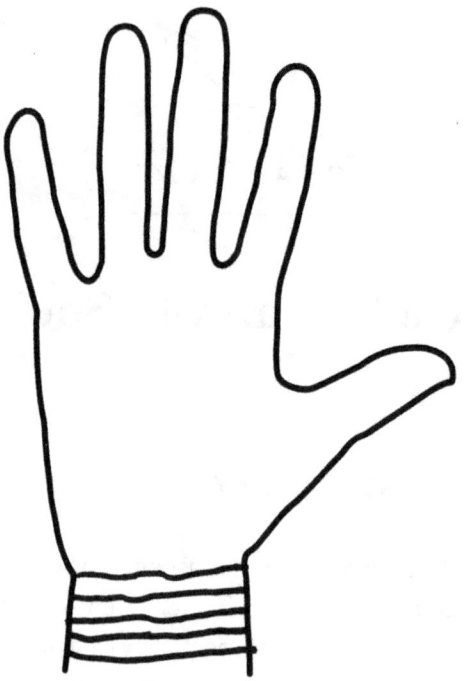

You should be especially aware of the topmost rascette, the one nearest the palm. If it is curved or broken on a woman's hand, it means health problems specific to females; on a male hand, it signals potential hormonal problems.

The rascettes, or horizontal lines, across the wrist indicate the number of lives that an individual has lived. Each rascette indicates periods of lives, more than just one. If there are four or more lines on your wrist, this is usually a strong indication of an old soul.

CHAPTER 24

Gain the Upper Hand

Being a Master Palmist has brought me many wonderful experiences. For example, at one expo, a woman sat down with me and had not one line or mark on her palm. That woman was passing away and had come to me asking the big question: what's next?

At other expos, I have seen many folks who have no career line in their palms, and when I explain to them that they have not come to do "career" but to experience multiple careers, they break into tears.

For, in our society, one of the first questions we ask our children is, "What are you going to be when you grow up?"

The rewards have been great, yet I offer a word of caution: to be a true palmist and reach the level of Master Palmist takes extreme study. While just a surface knowledge allows us to spot an individual's character strengths, we must be responsible in dispensing information. Without a wealth of learning and experience, there is a possibility of causing harm.

The most important idea I wish to leave with you is that in this life, we practice "free will." Consequently, no matter what your palms indicate, you always have the ability to change your mind and rearrange your life in a different direction.

Highlights of Palmistry

About the Author

Heidi E. Kent is a highly-experienced Master Palmist. Her psychic gifts of clairvoyance, clairaudience, and clairsentience were rigorously trained at the Spiritual Community of Camp Chesterfield where she received a diploma as a Certified Medium. Heidi also earned graduate degrees in psychology and museum studies, as well as additional certifications in her field.

Heidi has practiced the art of palm-reading throughout the United States and internationally from Europe to Mexico. She wrote *Highlights of Palmistry* to share her passion and expertise with readers in an easy and accessible way.

ENDNOTES

1. William G. Benham, *The Benham Book of Palmistry* (North Hollywood, California: Newcastle Publishing Co., Inc., 1988), 6.
2. Benham, *The Benham Book*, viii.
3. Benham, *The Benham Book*, viii.
4. Benham, *The Benham Book*, xiv, 7.
5. Benham, *The Benham Book*, xiv, 7.

REFERENCES/BIBLIOGRAPHY

Benham, William G. The Benham Book of Palmistry. North Hollywood, California: Newcastle Publishing Co., Inc., 1988.

Domin, Linda. *Instant Palm Reader*. St. Paul, Minnesota: Llewellyn Publications, 2000.

Jones, Katina Z. *The Everything Palmistry Book*. Avon, Massachusetts: Adams Media Corp., 2003.

Reid, Lori. *The Art of Hand Reading.* New York, New York: DK Publishing, Inc., 1996.

West, Peter. *The Complete Illustrated Guide to Palmistry.* New York, New York: Element Books Limited, 1998; Metro Books by arrangement with HarperCollins*Publishers*, Ltd., 2010.

IngramElliott Publishing

IngramElliott is an award-winning independent publisher with a mission to bring great stories to light in print and on-screen. We publish stories with a unique voice that will translate well into film, broadcast, and streaming television projects, as well as select non-fiction titles.

We look for a great story, unique voice, and the author's ability to build a strong platform. Please review our current submission guidelines and check out our latest releases.

www.ingramelliott.com

www.ingramcontent.com/pod-product-compliance
Lightning Source LLC
Chambersburg PA
CBHW062039120526
44592CB00035B/1438